W9-AHE-311

CODING IS EVERYWHERE

Coding in Computers

ELMHURST PUBLIC LIBRARY
125 S. Prospect Avenue
Elmhurst, IL 60126-3

by Elizabeth Noll

BELLWETHER MEDIA • MINNEAPOLIS, MN

Note to Librarians, Teachers, and Parents:

Blastoff! Readers are carefully developed by literacy experts and combine standards-based content with developmentally appropriate text.

Level 1 provides the most support through repetition of high-frequency words, light text, predictable sentence patterns, and strong visual support.

Level 2 offers early readers a bit more challenge through varied simple sentences, increased text load, and less repetition of high-frequency words.

Level 3 advances early-fluent readers toward fluency through increased text and concept load, less reliance on visuals, longer sentences, and more literary language.

Level 4 builds reading stamina by providing more text per page, increased use of punctuation, greater variation in sentence patterns, and increasingly challenging vocabulary.

Level 5 encourages children to move from "learning to read" to "reading to learn" by providing even more text, varied writing styles, and less familiar topics.

Whichever book is right for your reader, Blastoff! Readers are the perfect books to build confidence and encourage a love of reading that will last a lifetime!

This edition first published in 2019 by Bellwether Media, Inc.

No part of this publication may be reproduced in whole or in part without written permission of the publisher. For information regarding permission, write to Bellwether Media, Inc., Attention: Permissions Department, 6012 Blue Circle Drive, Minnetonka, MN 55343.

Library of Congress Cataloging-in-Publication Data

Names: Noll, Elizabeth, author.
Title: Coding in Computers / by Elizabeth Noll.
Description: Minneapolis, MN : Bellwether Media, Inc., 2019. | Series:
    Blastoff! Readers. Coding Is Everywhere | Includes bibliographical
    references and index. | Audience: Ages 5-8. | Audience: Grades K to 3.
Identifiers: LCCN 2017060022 (print) | LCCN 2017060778 (ebook) | ISBN
    9781626178335 (hardcover : alk. paper) | ISBN 9781618914774
    (pbk. : alk. paper) | ISBN 9781681035741 (ebook)
Subjects: LCSH: Programming languages (Electronic computers)–Juvenile literature.
Classification: LCC QA76.7 (ebook) | LCC QA76.7 .N65 2019 (print) | DDC 005.13–dc23
LC record available at https://lccn.loc.gov/2017060022

Editor: Christina Leaf   Designer: Brittany McIntosh

Printed in the United States of America, North Mankato, MN

Table of Contents

Coding in Computers

How do the computers in your home work?

They use a language made of 1s and 0s. This is called **binary code**.

Binary Letters

In binary code, "CODING IS FUN" looks like...

C 01000011   I 01001001
O 01001111   S 01010011
D 01000100   00100000
I 01001001   F 01000110
N 01001110   U 01010101
G 01000111   N 01001110
   00100000

Binary code is hard for humans to read. We invented special **programming languages** that are easier.

Computers can **translate** these into binary code.

Humans use programming languages to write **code**. Code tells the computer what to do.

Everything you do on a computer uses code. This could be typing your name or listening to music.

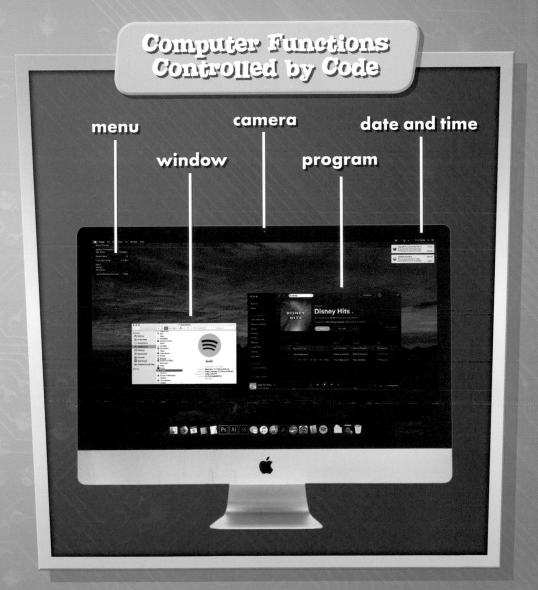

Computer Functions Controlled by Code

menu

camera

date and time

window

program

The History of Coding in Computers

Ada Lovelace

In 1843, Ada Lovelace wrote the first computer **program**.

Her friend invented a computing machine. Lovelace wrote notes on how it could work.

analytical engine computing machine

Programming became popular in the 1950s. Many people created new programming languages.

Grace Hopper, inventor of COBOL

learning
FORTRAN

FORTRAN solved math problems.
COBOL was easy to use.

Today, there are many more languages. They have made programming computers even easier.

Almost anyone can learn to code!

How Does Coding Work in Computers?

Code is like a recipe. You have to include every step.

1. Mix flour, baking powder, salt, and sugar
2. Stir in milk, egg, and butter
3. Pour batter into muffin tins
4. Put in oven at 350° for 25 minutes

If a step is missing or wrong,
the code will not work.

Say you want to listen to music. Code tells the computer to open the music program. It tells the program which song to play.

Listen to Music

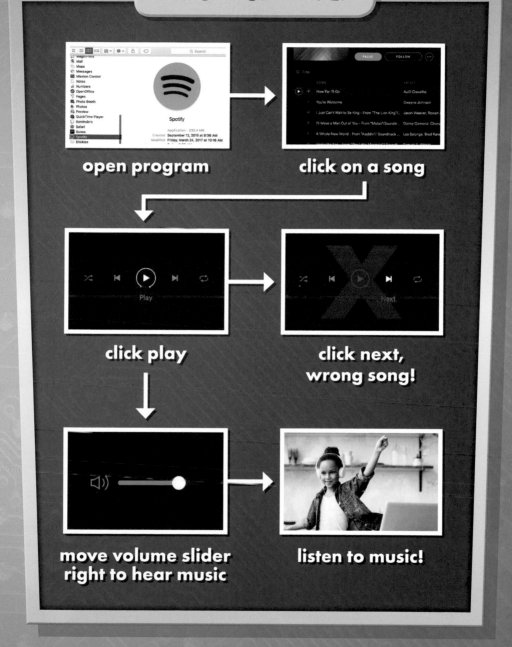

open program

click on a song

click play

click next,
wrong song!

move volume slider
right to hear music

listen to music!

Kids often learn to code with **Scratch** or **Blockly**.

Scratch

What kind of code would you write? You could create an **app** or a game that people love to play!

Glossary

app—a program for a cell phone or other mobile device

binary code—a language of 1s and 0s

Blockly—a simple visual programming language that is easy to learn

COBOL—an English-like programming language invented in 1959 that could work on many different machines; COBOL is short for common, business-oriented language.

code—instructions for a computer

FORTRAN—a programming language for science and math; FORTRAN is short for formula translation.

program—a set of rules for a computer that performs a specific function

programming languages—special languages that humans use to talk to computers

Scratch—a visual programming language that is easy to learn

translate—to turn words from one language into a different one

To Learn More

AT THE LIBRARY

Lyons, Heather. *Coding to Create and Communicate.*
Minneapolis, Minn.: Lerner Publications, 2018.

Stanley, Diane. *Ada Lovelace, Poet of Science: The
First Computer Programmer.* New York, N.Y.: Simon &
Schuster Books for Young Readers, 2016.

Wainewright, Max. *How to Code: A Step-by-Step
Guide to Computer Coding.* New York, N.Y.: Sterling
Publishing, 2016.

ON THE WEB

Learning more about
coding in computers is as
easy as 1, 2, 3.

1. Go to www.factsurfer.com.

2. Enter "coding in computers" into the search box.

3. Click the "Surf" button and you will see a
   list of related web sites.

With factsurfer.com, finding more information is
just a click away.

Index

The images in this book are reproduced through the courtesy of: Billion Photos, front cover; wavebreakmedia, p. 4; Ariel Skelley, p. 6; Rawpixel.com, p. 7; Africa Studio, p. 8; Brittany McIntosh, pp. 9, 19 (top left, top right, middle left, middle right, bottom left); Wikipedia, p. 10; De Agostini Editorial, p. 11; Science History Images, p. 12; Underwood Archives, p. 13; Phil's Mommy, pp. 14, 20; Hero Images, p. 15; NAR studio, p. 16; ERS Taylor, p. 17; KPG Payless2, p. 18; Kite_rin, p. 19 (bottom right); sturti, p. 21.